THE CONGO VOCABULARY IN CUBA

EGUIN FUNKÉ

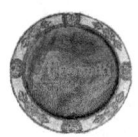

Copyright © 2009
All rights reserved.
ISBN:
https://www.orunmilaedition.com

Note to this Edition

The slave trade across the Atlantic, which lasted around three centuries, is estimated to have brought about a million slaves to Cuba. Most of it was carried out in the 19th century, mainly for work in the cane fields of the sugar mills.

A large crew arrived on the island during the year 1830, many of them coming from Sierra Leone located to the west of the African continent. Its name is an adaptation of the Portuguese version: Serra Leoa, whose meaning was "Sierra/Mountain Leone". During the 18th century it was an important center of the slave trade.

Once on the island, they were sold in some ports in western Cuba and many of them were placed directly in barracks specially built to house them in subhuman conditions, for which some perished due to the abusive mistreatment and hard work to which they were subjected.

In those battered barracks, the black slaves began to develop their rites and beliefs now adapted to the new conditions of habitat and slavery, mainly in the western and central regions of Matanzas Island, for example in the regions of Carlos Rojas, Jovellanos and Perico. This is how the groups called Gangas came together and every year in December they met to celebrate the Catholic festivities of syncretized San Lázaro and whom the Gangas call Yebbe, Kobayende, etc.

Although many healing secrets of the Gangas inherited from their ancestors from the Mokpangumba village tribe, many chants and rituals brought from that region are still preserved.

Some notes of songs and rites are preserved written in notebooks and manuscripts, which are transmitted from generation to generation.

A respect for the descendants of the Gangas precursors of these rules in Cuba such as: Emilio Ofarril Briyumba Congo; Zarabanda Nkita Munankita, Bustamante Siete Rayos, Bititi Sakampeño, Armando Palmer, Cheo Zarabanda, Zimba, etc.

Palo Monte, Palo Mayombe or Palo Quimbiza, arrived in Cuba with the slaves and settled in Havana, Regla Guanabacoa, Santiago de Cuba, Camagüey, Villa Clara, Sagua la Grande, etc.

So, this book constitutes a small contribution, so that the Afro-descendants of these latitudes can have a written testimony of the vocabulary used by their ancestors. And we have edited it with enough exemplary illustrations, so that people who speak English and other languages can easily identify the elements that are shown in this vocabulary.

THANKS

Thanks to all the Tata nkisi ke ti mbe lese Olodumare

Thanks to Siete Rayos for allowing me to make this book.

Thanks to the Congo ancestors' spirit, who came to Cuba as slaves.

Thanks to the spirit of Ta' Francisco "El Cagüeyo" who always accompanies and guides me.

CONTENT

Chapter 1 p.

Congo Alphabet--------------------------------------1

Congo Vocabulary ---------------------------------2 to 42

Episode 2

Bantu Vocabulary for Ritual Use in Cuba------43 to 56

Chapter 3

Photos to illustrate the Congo in Cuba vocabulary—57 to 135

CHAPTER 1

CONGO ALPHABET

A..................... ....Yugo
B...Yulo
C...Yili
CH...Busipa
D...E Buo
E...D Saluari
F...Came
G...Bisula
H..................... ....Busili
I...Tiluli
J... Yalumi
K...Talaba
L...Bi
LL...Biubi
M...Duli
N...Suli
Ñ...Balu
P...Dilonia
Q...Oou
R...Yolito
RR...Timini
S...Yurico
T...Halua
U...Simbulu
V...Sume
X...Nvi
Y...Tense
Z...Huiton

CONGO VOCABULARY.

Angoya: Cane of the foundation that is danced when there is GUARANDOYA. Which is delivered sealed in its union.

Anafinda: Savannah.

Akara: Husband.

Ague mene: Today.

Airosa kinoni: Ice.

Ajimo: Belly.

Akueto: The opposite.

Akure: Right.

Alango: The hill.

Ampambia: Big brother.

Ankere: Bad.

Andilanga: Distant times.

Atizala: Hide.

Aviankan: Osain.

Azolo: Wind.

Azumbo: The mountain.

Anagongo: Sesame

Ashiviriki: Miguel Archangel.

Sharpen: Hide.

Ando Bay Kebo: That you doubt.

Amputo: Lego.

Akuton Bile: Cook.

Anene: Great.

Atakoko: Because of my grandfather.

Aribu Bombaya: Evil spirits.

Ankuta: Food of the dead or the nkisi.

Amuana: Cemetery ceremony.

Ankomengane: Unknown face.

Amanigunda: Inverted woman.

Ariongo: Current of the river.

Asualo: Spirit of the mouth of the river.

Aterere: Excuse me.

Avianzan: Gurufinda.

B

Babula: Unleash.

Babulu - Ngurufinda: The one who possesses the spirit of an ancestor.

Bakonfula: Steward. Ganga's son

Bakuso: Damn.

Basheshe: Strong.

Bade: What it is not.

Badeselva: Dance.

Bandome: Dark colors. Red wine.

Bafiote: Black.

Bakasala: Clapping.

Bakufa: Garment butler.

Bakuende Bomban: San Antonio.

Bakuyere: Husband.

Baluande Kiambiko: God of the Sea.

Baluandi: Virgin of Regla.

Baluka: Change your mind.

Bambo: Tribe.

Bane: Punches.

Bandoki: Warlock

Bandu: Broth.

Banduina: Flag.

Bango: Last.

Bangundo: Crocodile.

Bankita: Ancestors.

Baombo: Bitter Broom.

Barabadio: San Pedro.

Barabanda: San Pedro.

Barakuame: Hat.

Baralondinga: Tell something.

Basagara: Palm of the hand.

Basala langueto: Back of the hand.

Basame kakulango: Running water.

Basangal: Palm of the hand.

Batalla: Air.

Batato Bongo: A Governor.

Batente: Stick to give.

Bati: All that......

Bebe: Lips.

Bebe sinfe: White Clothes.

Bemba: The Cacayda.

Bembo Nula: Cloud Tail.

Benwa: Cyclone.

Bekele: Inflamed liver.

Bibamance: Corojo butter.

Bibiosima: Fire Ant.

Bikan biko: That they are not abandoned, interrupted, finished, change.

Bishishi: Bug.

Bishishi meko: Worm.

Bigan diame: Elements used to make the ngangas.

Bikongo luango: Royal Cone.

Bilongo: Witchcraft.

Biga: Find out, search.

Biningulo: Pig.

Binsin sunsu: Rooster meat.

Bioko: See, look.

Biroburo: Talkative.

Bisi: Meat, eggs (Animals).

Bisonse: Clove.

Bisonse bukilanga: Line nail.

Bisonse bukilanga endumba: Clove.

Bisonse ensusu: Cock Spur.

Bisongo: Clove.

Bisonsi: Fish.

Bisuri: Nose.

Bitondo: Stinky.

Boata: Bottle.

Bobe: Kiss.

Bobelankele: Thunder.

Bofiate: Mulatto.

Boileo: Stroke that is left at the foot of a tree, represents another self in his life.

Boime: Staff.

Bolocka: Peseta.

Boma: I roll.

Bombofinda: Elephant.

Bomba: Maja, jar, tie strong.

Bomb la Bumpar: Cat.

Boma: Old pestle with jars.

Bonda: Cast.

Bonke: Honey from bees.

Bonsa Limpa: Field.

Bubokoka: Peacock.

Bukilanda: Railroad.

Bumo: stomach.

Bun: Go away.

Bunonfoka: The night.

Bundo Basonde: Banana soup.

Bungonda: Chinese.

Bunke: Honey of Bees.

Bukilanga: Railroad.

Burubbano: Old.

Burukuame: Hat.

Burukuntela: Fight, problem.

Brankanioni: Balls, testicles

Strong Arm: San Cristóbal.

Bria: Food, Fall.

Briyumba: Land where the first Nkisi, Manbe, lived.

Brimine: Pulse, ring.

C

Cangari: Rhinoceros.

Caboronda: Police.

Cashikauhal: Chair or seat.

Cafu: Caravel.

Caffo: Crowd.

Caffu: Meeting.

Caffunyo: Partner.

Calaza: Pumpkin.

Calunga: Mar.

Cayesu: It's dirty.

Campo finda: Cemetery.

Camarioka: Chameleon.

Canda: Letter or paper.

Candango: Clay pot.

Cangre: Yucca.

Carao: Damn.

Carcoma: Bibijaguas.

Cariampemba: Meeting of three.

Carire: Heck, star or two.

Carike: King of what never dies.

Catuka: Machuca.

Caye: This.

Centella: Oya.

Cisele: Tooth.

Co: No or From.

Cocoansa: River.

Conwoko: Dude.

Congwame: He doesn't love me.

Conguso: Ass.

Congo: Head.

Condia: Pumpkin.

Conboka: Go up.

Consuako: Compadre.

Confinda: Field.

Coromina: Spider.

Coralillo: Creeper.

Cota: Bury.

Cotalemba: Cemetery.

Cu: you.

Cuba: Die or finish.

Cuaco: Laughter.

Cuako cuako: Mocking laugh.

Cuadrilla: Group or family.

Cuama: Take.

Cuame kiako: disturb little.

Cuananwao: East.

Cuane: Annoy.

Cuatro Vientos (Four winds): Eleguá.

Cobayende (Kobayende): Saint Lazarus.

Cuko: Coconut.

Cukuako: Compadre.

Cukuaen Cuaki: At dawn.

Cuenda ko: Come in, come in, come.

Cueto: We are.

Cueto endioko: We are great.

Cuguenfiata: Saint Benedict of Palermo.

Cuile: Necklace.

Cuilo: Bird.

Cumbe: Chariot

Cuna: Sabana, something that sprouts, is born.

Cunalombo: Las Villas.

Cunalombo: Daylight.

Cunalumbo: Heaven.

Cunayanda: Well.

Cunayaonda: Far Land.

Cunambanza: Havana.

Cunambata: Get up.

Cunanfinda: Jungle.

Cunanguako: Your mother's pussy.

Cunansimba: Jungle.

Cunanshila: From the heart.

Cunansieto: Matanzas.

Cunankisa: Santa Catalina.

Cundo: He wants to.

Cuni: Stick.

Cunia: Tree.

Cunofinda: Savannah.

Cunonsulo: Heaven.

Cutare: Blessing.

Cutukuonkala: Gourd.

Cuturilan: Protection.

Cuyerere: Cocuyo.

Cligaringa: Gorroneo.

Cruye: Split or break.

Ch

Chacuana Eneco: Saint Lazarus.

Chala: Spoon.

Chamalongo: Four pieces of coconut.

Chamba: Drink of the foundation.

Chaulende: Chinese.

Chea: Smoke.

Cheshe: Good.

Cheshe basheshe: Very strong.

Chesherewanko: Pitirre.

Chesheregoma: Cricket

Antiagola. 3rd Drum: Music from the mountain that was brought to the BRIYUMBA land by the Mandingas as an offering to the Mambe festival.

Chesherenwara: La Garza.

Chesheremapiango: Deer.

Cheshere Guanga: Tomeguin.

Chetundie: Wise.

Chi: Leon.

Chikombe: Jutia.

Chikirimato: Attention.

Chimirimoto: Open your ears.

Chola nwenwe: Caridad del Cobre.

Cholo: Toad.

Chula: Toad.

Chulun: Bembe, Congo King of Africa.

D

Deyini: Breasts.

Dialanga: Handkerchief.

Diambe: Dia.

Diambulanga: He is lost.

Dian: In, and, why, what.

Diana: War.

Dianfula: Tempest.

Diamati: From the heart.

Dilanga: Past tense.

Diloso: Rice.

Dimanwe: Scratch, write.

Dinga: say, give.

Dudomebibiosima: Thunder.

Dundu: Ghost.

Doke: Better, it's a leg of the foundation.

E

Eki: Sacrifice.

Elefano: Elephant.

Elice: Lucero.

Elana: Spider.

Emba: Trace.

Eembala: Sweet potato.

Embania: Poison.

Embak: Dwarf.

Embele: Machete.

Embeleto: Razor.

Embembo: African.

Emboma: Snake.

Embongo: Boy.

Embuenwe: Carious.

Embuga: Speak.

Empaka: Prepared jar.

Empaloto: Color.

Empanwe: Brother.

Empaso: Son.

Empemba: Sail.

Empolo: Powder.

Empopo: Brain.

Empungo: Power.

Enkandia: Skin or skin.

Enkobo: Snail.

Enkombo: Body.

Enkombo mene: Goat.

Enkombo Su: Ass.

Enkuele: Enter.

Enkumbe: Cart.

Enkumbe washilanga: Bus (bus).

Enkumbe kalunga: Boat.

Enkuna: Trust.

Enkuto: Hear, ear.

Enshila Sefua: World.

Endelín: San Antonio.

Endia: Tripe.

Endiata: Traitor.

Endinga: Say or ask.

Endioko: Big.

Endioko Embogo: Great.

Endoba: Kill.

Enduki: Hot pepper.

Endundo: Ghost.

Endumba: Woman.

Endundo: Albino.

Finda: Mount.

Enfita: Lily.

Enfiuri: Go away.

Enfuka: Fever, night.

Enfumbe: Dead.

Enfuri: Spirit.

Engando batalla: Caiman.

Engo: Tiger.

Engombe: Bull.

Engonda: Moon.

Engongoro: Jicotea.

Enguey: Dia.

Engulo: Pig.

Engumbiro: Centipede.

Engundo liri: Palma.

Enkanda: Letter.

Enkewe: Monkey.

Enkele: Star.

Enkelekundo: God willing.

Enkere: Left.

Enketo: Mulatto.

Enkunia: Tree.

Enlonga: Bath.

Enniete: Good.

Emina: From behind.

Enkiete: Up.

Ensara: Work.

Ensaranda: Spell.

Ensasi: Lightning.

Ensefo: Hair.

Ensendi: Cheek.

Ensere: Nfumbe hair.

Ensila: Path.

Ensilako: Walking.

Ensimba: Leon.

Ensulo: Heaven.

Ensunga: Tobacco.

Ensunga mundele: Cigar.

Ensunga nayembe: Mariuna.

Ensuso batalla: Ceiba.

Ensuso kobayende: Guinean.

Ensuso damba: Owl.

Ensuso ganga: Rooster.

Eensuso huanamburo: Duck.

Ensuso indumba: Chicken.

Ensuso Liwe: Guinea.

Ensuso mambo: Peacock.

Ensuso sambia: Dove.

Ensuso suao: Duck.

Entanda: Tongue.

Entango: Sun.

Entiete: Jícara.

Ento: Front.

Entombre: Caña Brava.

Endele: Stop.

Entokokalunga: Earth, Sea.

Entuala: Cat.

Entufi: Shit.

Entumba Urialango: Glass.

Entumbo: Bottle.

Entun: Belly.

Enyere: King.

Endioko Embogo: Great.

Engaging Battle: Alligator.

Endoki: Ghost.

Enkoki: Arrow.

Engando Vititi: Toad.

Enkueye: Holy.

Entosato: Deer.

Entebo: bow arrow.

Entana: Away.

Engembo: Bat.

Enguardia: Hypocrite.

Endoyi: Dream.

Ensosa: Chain.

Enkuaye: Monkey.

Entoto Carcoma: Bibijagua Land.

Entoto Siafna: Land of the Dead.

Entoto ko Ierí: Tierra Palama.

Entoto ko Talemba: Cemetery Land.

Entoto ko Embembo: African Land.

Entoto ko Chaulende: Chinese Land.

Entoto ko Kalunga: Land Sea.

Entoto ko Suansa: Land River.

Entoto ko Iyansila: Land of 4 Paths.

Entoto ko Finda: Mount Earth.

Entoto ko Guadilonga: Guardarraya Land.

Entoto ko kuna: Tierra Loma.

Entoto ko Joromina: Anthill Land.

Enhiso: Time.

Enhiso Pengala: Dry season.

Enhiso mamba: Rainy season.

Enhiso Kinoni: Cold season.

F
Falla: Candela.

Fatuwame: Belly.

Finda: Mt.

Finda anabuto: Center of the mount.

Floron: Fabric.

Frusunga: To smoke tobacco.

Frusungamundale: Cigar smoking.

Funca: Night.

Fua: He died.

Fua Menso: Blind.

Fusenda: False, it doesn't work.

Fua Nkuto: Deaf.

Fua Nchila: Mute.

Fula: Gunpowder.

Fula Inoka: Storm.

Fuim Batalla: Horn without charging.

G

Gambula: Whirlpool.

Gambalenwe: Doctor.

Gambuleso: Bad Wind.

Ganao: Astro.

Gando: Beings or elements that had or have movable life.

Gando Siro: dry güiro.

Gando Cueva: Crocodile.

Gganga: Fundamental casserole.

Ggangula: Light.

Gganga Entare: Blacksmith.

Gato: Sparrowhawk.

Giabola: Grandma.

Gonda: Moon.

Gongori: Mayor.

Gongoro: Jicotea.

Gua: Yes.

Guabilonga: Guardarraya.

Guayigun: Leprosy.

Guandí: Soursop.

Guano: Pants.

Guao: Dog.

Guariguari: False, gossipy, talkative.

Guarilonga: Current.

Guarandoya: War.

Guariao: Burial.

Guariere: Guardian.

Guarandonga: Party or meeting of fundamentals to work.

Guatoko: Child.

Guba: Bean.

Gubasambi: Chickpea.

Guba Zarabanda: Colorados.

Guba Bafiote: Blacks.

Guba Kindiame: Little face.

Gubatu: Chicharo.

Guba Mundele: beans.

23

Guembo: Fingers.

Guembo Garire: Bat.

Gueta: Time.

Guiri Mambo: Sing.

Guisa: Night.

Gumbembe: Jutia.

Gumbele: Eat.

Gunda: Bell.

Guesa: Smell.

I
Imba: I sing.

Ina: Nine (9).

Ina: Light.

Ina Ensasi: Lightning Lightning.

Ina Gonda: Moonlight.

Ina Mundale: Electric Light.

Ina Nkele: Star Light.

Ina Tango: Sunlight.

Ina ko Diambe: Daylight.

Indimuana: Miss.

Indumba: Woman.

J

Jamba: Statue.

Janda: Down.

Jole: Stick doll.

Jole ko Muenda: Plaster doll.

Jorumina: Ant.

Jurutimba: Bug that has mayimbe that knocks down the hair.

Kabanka: House of Africa on NKITA land to
  banks of the Congo River. Strong for resisting the floods of this river.

Kabialanga: Guardarraya, threshing floor.

Kaduko: Something old.

Kala: It will do. live or be

Kalampemba: It's going to make you dead.

Kalunga: Mar.

Kamakeke: Trap.

Kana Amene: When something happens.

Kanagandi: Face bone.

Kanga: Tie up.

Kanga yana: Tie here.

Kansu: River water.

Karire: Hugs. Eternal.

Karulenda: Dead man who lives in the mountains, is the one who clears the road to EMBUA.

Kasikawala: Altar with tiger skin.

Kiako: Walking.

Kiakolumene: Little by little.

Kianko: Little.

Kiangana: Running:

Kigembombembo: Whirlwind.

Kikiri: Star.

Kikoroto: San Francisco.

Kiyumba: House of the Dead.

Kiyise: Bone.

Kimbansa: Weeds.

Kimbanza: First procession or Cabildo that came out in Africa for the way of greeting the Sun and the stars, so that the initiates could see it.

Kimbula: Song of Pullas.

Kimpenso: Storm.

Kimpunwele: Give me strength.

Kinamputo: Coconut shell.

Kinduila: Cross yourself.

Kindembo: Iron pot.

Kindiam: Family.

Kinfuiti: Drum of the dead that bellows.

Kingenko: Gavilan.

Kisenwele: Fundamental secret. River fly.

Kisenwere: Quill of death.

Kisiac: Foundation.

Kisiambela: Change voice.

Kisidia: The only thing.

Kisonde: Bun.

Kitempolo: Evil rain.

Ko: no.

Koko Wansa: Center of the river.

Konwako: Dude.

Konko: Holy ban.

Kontagri: Ceremony for the elderly with the skin of the tiger.

Konyose: Pact.

Kota Lemba: Cemetery.

Kotoroto: Parrot.

Kuana: Pull.

Kuame: Go away, I'm leaving.

Kubonda: Kill.

Kukamba: Pain.

Kuenda: Enter.

Kunalombo: The Villas.

Kunalongo: Cemetery, drinks that are taken in the consecrations of the elders.

Kunayanda: Africa.

Kunan: Blessing.

Kunanbanza: Havana.

Kunantoliya: Cemetery.

Kunsa: River.

Kura: Well, us.

Kutenewere: Voice.

Ll
LLamboso (Jamboso): Drink of the Foundation
LLento (Jento): Us.
LLijo (Jiho): Son.
LLinbula (Jimbula): Feast
LLisombe Jisombe): The glory.
LLonco (Jonko): Sit down

L
Lamputa: Lightning.

Lamberito: Cleaning.

Lango: Water.

Lango Shola: River Water.

Lango gulo: Butter.

Lango Mayimbe: Eagle.

Lango Kisonde: Pee.

Lango Mundele: Milk.

Lango Pielewa: Coffee.

Lango Zambi: Rainwater.

Lango NKisi: Holy Water.

Lan: Crazy.

Lano: Donkey.

Lega: Sleep.

Lele: Egg.

Lembé: Dead.

Lenwe: Chest.

Liguena: lizard, slug.

Licombola: Knee.

Lifangude: Leg.

Linga: Singar.

Liri: Oshosi.

Lombo: Day.

Longoya: Doodle.

Loyo: Life, Bone.

Lubbe: White skinned.

Luka: Go on.

Luka Emba: Follow trail.

Lukambe: 3 devils.

Lukameasi: 3 devils.

Lukaemba: 3 devils.

Lukananwere: Go Straight.

Lukansi: Lucifer.

Lukena: Live head.

Lucero Mundo: Eleguá.

Lukuana: Flowers.

Lufrusunga: You smoke tobacco.

Lumbamba: boss.

Lumbe: Candela.

Lumene: Wait.

Lumene Masimene: Wait till tomorrow.

Lungando: Devil.

Lusankuara: Rainbow.

Lusuala: Feathers.

Lutete: Star.

Lutunga: Eye disease.

M
Ma: Things.

Makaka: Coconut.

Makujende: Guanajo.

Makulo: Protection.

Makundo: Banana.

Makala: Woman.

Makala Kasha: Basin.

Makate: Shit.

Malafo sese: Dry wine.

Malafo nputo: Aguardiente.

Malafo Uria Balbande: Melao.

Malafo Uria Chola: Honey.

Malafo Uria Ganga: Chamba.

Malafo Uria Sambi: Red wine.

Maleke: Pumpkin.

Malembe: Slow down, bad.

Mama Nyaweji: Mother Serpent.

Mamba: Water.

Mamba Kalunga: Sea Water.

Mamba Singula: It's going to rain.

Mamboto: Mix.

Mana: Comply.

Manawenwe: Las Mercedes.

Mandondo: Worm.

Manfula: Resurrection.

Manganioni: Fagot.

Mankuala: Hand.

Mankenkere: Child.

Manunfuka: Mother night.

Masabieke: Wise, knowledgeable.

Masango: Protection.

Masango Nsara: Corn straw.

Masango Uria: Corn flour.

Masimene: Tomorrow.

Masimene Pandiane: Tomorrow I come.

Mataka: Buttock.

Matako: Like.

Matako Lukaye: How are you?

Matari: Stone.

Matari Nsasi: Lightning stone.

Matende Bane: Stick to hit.

Maune: Omelette.

Mayanga: Priest.

Mayimbe: Tiny.

Mayunga: Cheer up alone.

Mbumba kifuite: Mother of Nnoca.

Mekate: Bun.

Meleto: Melón.

Membo: Finger.

Menga: Blood.

Mensu: Look, see.

Miapao: Bread.

Mina: Back.

Misuri: Nose.

Mite: Saliva.

Moko: Hand, arm.

Mojiganga: Chichiricú.

Monga Kalunga: Salt.

Mono: Me.

Moomba: Rotten.

Mosembo: Learn.

Mu: Me, me.

Muana: Man or Mother.

Muana Gecola: Little boy.

Muenda: Plaster.

Mumba: Witchcraft.

Mumbala: Sweet potato.

Mumua: Mouth.

Munanfinda: Savannah.

Munanwenwe: Las Mercedes.

Munansi Ntufi: Excused.

Munanso: House.

Munanso wanabeto: Jail.

Munanso Kuni kafeoti: Charcoal.

Munanso Mandele: Dairy.

Munanso Naibola: Temple.

Munanso Sambi: Church.

Munanso Uria: Winery.

Munanso Uria Ngombe: Butcher shop.

Mundele: White.

Munica a: Ram.

Muraya: Jail.

Murunwana: Foreigner.

Musenga: Sugar.

Mutangoe Mutic: First Mask.

N
Na: Goes.

Nakala: It will do.

Nébelé: Machete.

Nébele Kasuso: Knife.

Nbele Sambele: African Machete.

Nébelo: Man.

Ncembo: Body.

Nkuyo: Good Spirit.

Ndoki: Evil Spirit.

Nikuako: Arm.

Nkay: Mulatto.

Nketo Mayaola: Chinese.

Nsambi Liri: Children of God.

Nsansa: Wood.

Nsatu: Hungry.

Ntanwe: Hollow that is made under the foundation.

Ñ
Ñoka: Snake

O
Ofuna: Ceiba.

Ofuna: Wind.

Osototo Mundale: Rice

P
Pachangara: Tortillera.

Palmiche: Broom.

Panwanarere: Bird.

Panwiamate: Shoes.

Panwiaree: Feet.

Patipuanza: Saint Lazarus.

Patiyaga: Saint Lazarus.

Pemba Keto: Pencil.

Piango Piango: Little by little.

Pikuti: Little.

Plan: Banana.

Test Strength: Eleguá.

Q

Quianko Quianko: Little by little.

Quiangana: Eat.

Quiako Lumene: Wait a bit.

Quiankuloco: Dwarf.

Quiendiambo: Who is it?

Quiendiembo: Fundamental room.

Quilanga: Who are you, what does it bring?

Quilokoto: Crying or rain.

Quiyenga: Milk.... pa.

Quimbanza: Yerba.

Quinani: Name.

Quini: Search.

Quintomble: Cloud.

Quinseto: Bless.

S
Sa: This.

Sakiriri: Seven Stars.

Samba: Scream.

Sambia Nfuiri NKisi: Holy Spirit.

Sambi: God.

Sambiempungo: Power of God.

Sambi Lukutare: God bless you.

Sambi Munantoto: God of Earth.

Sambi Munansulo: God of the Sky.

Sambi Munansulo: God of the Congo.

Sambrano Sasi: Seven Rays.

Sance: Spirit.

Sanga: Dance.

Santico: Name.

Sara: One.

Sarabana: Saint Peter.

Sarasano: Long ago.

Sefila: He died.

Sefua Nkuto: Deaf.

Sila: Walk.

Simbra: Tremble.

Sinato: Alone, unique.

Sincere: Freedom.

Syngoma: Drum.

Sinsoriwe: Pain.

Sinkeiloka: Neck.

Sivinicunankuasa: Spirit of the river.

Soba: traditional chief.

Somba: Fruit.

Sopay: Okra.

Soyanga: They are bugs.

Su: Dirty.

Susana: River.

SuKuenda: Take care.

T
Taita: Grandpa.

Talankera: Door.

Tambua iya erumbo: Whirlpool 4 winds.

Tana: Orange.

Tango: Sun.

Tarambele: Close.

Tari: Bed.

Tata Jiabolo (a): Grandfather (a).

Tata Nkisi: Godfather of garment.

Tato: Three (3).

Teite: Jícara.

Tegué: Chichiricú.

Tente: Jump.

Terekunta: Ram.

Teremende: Deer.

Tilla: Broom.

Earth Tremble: Mercedes.

Tokuanto: Pitirre.

Tondele: Hold on.

Tuine: Guasasa.

Rumba Tomb: Strong Wind.

Tumbara: High.

Tulumba: True.

U
Uria: Food.

Uriando: Eaten.

Uriar: Eat.

V
Vana: Here.

Vanta: Get up.

Vanta Nkambo: Raise body.

Vene: Mouth.

Viyaya (Biyaya): Mystery.

Viyayango: Fundamental Secret.

Vioko (Bioko): Eye, see, look.

Vititi (Bititi): See monte.

Vititi Menso (Bititi Menso): Looking North.

Vuelta Ngonda: Clock.

W
Wow: what.

  Wuatako: Child.

  Wowso: Egg.

  Wuiriko: Hey.

  Wuisa: They turn on.

Y
Yaba: Guava.

  Yambele: Sabre.

  Yari Yari: Illness.

Yay: Bad.

Yaji: Mother.

Yimbila: Bird Song.

Yimbula: Feast.

Yole: Stick doll.

Yyute: Straw.

Yuyumbila: Black Cloak.

Z
Zansa: Wood.

Zarabanda: Saint Peter.

Zimbo: Money.

Zun: Pinwheel

CHAPTER 2

BANTÚ VOCABULARY OF RITUAL USE IN CUBA

A

Abrir:	Sabule.
Acabar:	Mona.
Acto Sexual:	Makate tisonda.
Agua que se hecha en la calle con fines mágicos:	Guria nsila.
Acusar:	Funde.
Agua:	Nomba longo.
Agua bendita:	Longo sombria.
Aguardiente:	Malafo.
Aguardiente de corojo:	Malafonmabo.
Animal salvaje:	Kiana.
Amarre:	Kanguila.
Aprender:	Tuna kiongo.
Árbol:	Nkumi.
Arrodillarse:	Kukona.
Asunto:	Diamba.
Asiento:	Muanda.
Atar:	Kange.
Atar fuerte:	Bomba.
Azúcar:	Suikisi.

B

To dance:	Kuambe.
Flag:	Dimbri.
Belly:	Munalusa.
Women's robe:	Matute.
Battle:	Nduona.
Foundation Drink:	Kimbisa, chomba.
Bug:	Munfuira.
White:	Mundele.
Creole white:	Mundele mafuita.
Mustache:	Nsuosu.
Mouth:	Mia-mua.
Battle:	Ntombo, boota.
Apothecary:	Ganga lembe.
Arm:	Lembo, nikuanko, leko.
Witchcraft:	Ngari.
Sorcerer:	Mangatere.
good warlock:	Enganga sombi.
bad warlock:	Nganga-ndoki.
Sorcerer Warlock:	Nkonga nukonga.
Bundle:	Kite.
Search find out:	Bingun.

C

Horse:	Kumbe.
Head:	Munontu.
Head back started:	Muona ntutugonga.
mad dog head	Muona ntu kiyumba.
String:	Lukomba.
Town hall:	Luna.
Fall out:	Bria.

Skull:	Ntu.
Fever:	Nfuka.
Heat:	Nsapeka.
Wear:	Mata.
Bed:	Nfula.
Path:	Psila, hsila.
Mountain path:	Asila kima nfinda.
Countryside:	Bonsa limpia.
Bell:	Kuela bembo.
Song:	Nkunga.
Candle:	Mbarco.
dirge:	Nbembo.
Canyon:	Matende.
Expensive:	Mua sala.
Coal:	Etra, ekale, mekale.
Jail:	Nso zarabanda.
Meat:	Mbisi.
Pork meat:	Bikaliote.
Rooster meat:	Binsin sunsu.
Letter – paper:	Nkoda.
Stuff:	Nso.
Married:	Kuela.
Casserole:	Kuya.
Warlock Casserole:	Ngarori.
Cemetery:	Campo nfinda, kariempeba, kabalongo, kumunso fumbi, malon, bosa lombajosa, dieto, punun surva, noso fuir, kumangongo, sakimakue, kombombinda nfianda, nso fua.
Ash:	Kumbre.
Wax:	Ndimbre.
Cyclone:	Tombula.

Sky: Nsulo.
Waist: Murrila nkueto.
Cook: Akuto bile.
Elbow: Kingonia.
Color: Blanco mfemba.
Color: Muindo.
Necklace: Nsanga.
Eat: Ndia, urdiar.
Partner: Mundonguelle.
actual cone: Bikongo luango.
Set of magic sticks or branches: Nkunia.
Black colour: Bandombe, ndombe.
Talkative: Nisa uipabo.
summon - avoid: kuta.
Heart: Nchila, tua, tuma.
Cut: Kanda.
Electric current: Ngungula.
Cold: Nkuru.
Grow up: Elula nkula.
Creole: Mambuto.
Neck: Singue eloka.
Knife: Mbete koto.
Knife - machete: Mebele.
Medicine man: Nganga muno.
Curious: Kuna kosi.

D

Dance: Kina.
Dantu dance: Makuba.
Give to the drum: Ribetear.
Finger. Lembo, lolembo.

God of the sea.	Baluande, kalungo.
Iron god.	Zarabanda.
Tie off:	Babula.
Slowly:	Molenbe.
Behind:	Kumanina.
Day:	Lumbo.
Tooth:	Menus.
Tell me:	Quirino.
Direction:	Nkembo.
Money:	Mbonro, simbo.
Gave:	Lumbo.
God:	Ampungo, nsambi.
Shadow:	Sambrianpungo.
God who brings luck:	Simbi.
To sleep:	Leka.
Great God of Heaven:	Tubisi nsombi.
Great God of the Earth:	Mpugun sambi.

E

Them:	Yao.
Them:	Kua.
Loved:	Yambisa.
Sick:	Yori.
Palm nut broom:	Komba.
Star:	Siempre telbe.
Dwarf:	Nkufi.
Disease:	Yeye.
To teach:	Longa.
enter, go:	Kuendo.
Climb:	Mounda kombe.
Hide:	Sueka.
The mountain:	Kunonfinda, nefanda

	onabutu sabona ngeme.
Shotgun:	Nguela.
evil spirit:	Miense, tete.
Foreign:	Lugunda.
Great:	Mbora.
The oldest:	Mbuta.
The sun rises:	Tengo isa.

F

Favor:	Nsopeka.
Cold:	Finfi.
Bottom of the sea.	Nfunda Kolunga.
Stove:	Maka.
Strong:	Jakuma, kungalo.

G

Governor:	Fumuabate, atabongo.
Blow:	Mbula.
Thank you:	Ndolele.
Great:	Anene.
Cluster:	Lumbi.
Hoe:	Nsongo.

H

Speaks:	Mbaba.
Talk loud:	Tubula mdige.

Snake room: Munonso mbena.
Cornmeal: Mpalo masongo.
Female: Ndumba.
Brother: Ngueyo, mpague, panguiame, nfongo.
Child: Kunje kale.
Daughter, girl: Muona kento.
Tree leaves: Nkondon lele.
Men: Zakara.
White man: Mundele.
Big man: Mantu yo pene.
Hospital: Kuasa munansa.
Today: Kuanke.
Bone: Muensi.
dead bone: Konkoma.
Egg: Nui.
savannah bird egg: Nuinibalele.

I

Language: Ndinge.
Church: Munonso nfunbala.
Initiated: Ngueyo.
Intestine: Ndia.
Go, come, come: Guise.
Left: Onkento.

J

Gourd: Cutukuonkala.
Jimagua: Nsibonsilea.
Young: Matojo nkeyo.

49

Jew (a) (non-Christian): Ndoki.

L

The capital:	Kumanbasa.
Havana:	Kumbansa.
The Manigua:	Sabana ngombe.
The monkeys:	Lembo.
Whip:	Musinga.
Place:	Tula.
Far:	Kuna ntema.
Language:	Tonoa.
Book:	Nkuko.
Clean up:	Sukula.
Cleaning:	Nsala.
Knoll:	Mongo.
The feet:	Pondiambe.
Moon:	Ngonda, nguando.
Full moon:	Ngonda, nguóndo.
Light:	Mini.
Crazy:	Sabi nturí.
Moonlight:	Mieso.
Sore:	Nauta.
Cry:	Pita.
Rain:	Nfula ndaka.

M

Husband:	Yakele, yakara.
Machete:	Embele.
Male:	Yukala.
Wood:	Nti.

Mother:	Yaya, kiondi.
Godmother:	Tikan tikan.
Early morning:	Makurere,
Bow:	Neko.
Send:	Mondo, matado.
mount of corojo:	Masinguese, masi, maba.
cocoa butter:	Mosi guengo.
Tomorrow:	Mosimene.
Garment Steward:	Bakufa.
Mace:	Kumabonbo
Medicine:	Nlongo.
Cheeks:	Efendi.
Liar:	Wari, nguonguia.
Loves me:	Nkebele.
Fear:	Boma.
Shit:	Ntufi.
Watch:	Menús, bititi.
Mystery:	Mbumba.
Mountain:	Kumonfunda, kumamfinda.
To bite:	Tateka.
Young guy:	Kuruban, monkereré.
A lot of money:	Mbonga, mbala.
Dead:	Fua.
Dead:	Nfumbe.
Woman:	Muana.
White woman:	Muana mundele.
Naked woman:	Muana katuto kumulele.
Honest woman:	Ndumba yalea.
Woman without child:	Nkentonsile.
Mulatto:	Boniato, bofiate.
Musician:	Pungui

N

Buttocks: Mataka.
Nose: Nsasuri.
Razor: Mbele sambi.
Black: Nketo.
Black by birth: Ndombo mbembo.
No: Gongome.
New: Maki.

O

Dark: Lombo, tombe.
Ear: Kuto.
deaf ear: Fuomoto.
Eyes: Menso, diso.
Ear: Kutu, katp, akuto.
Sexual organ (female): Ndino, nkuto wiri.

P

Land of the dead: Nsige si nfua.
Dad: Tatandi, onabutu.
Stick dressed in skirts that feeds like Elegua: Ariku bombaya.
Handkerchief: Diareso.
Paper: Nfunda.
umbrella: Talongo.
Intestinal parasite: Adiangelolo.
Give birth: Buta.
Dog with eyes: Guanomenso.
Temple: Nsapo.
Chest: Nturopene, kata, mokate.
pawn dog: Yimbi, yakara.

Stone:	Matari.
lightning stone:	Matari Isasi, matari mukiona, matari yille.
Lodestone:	Songue.
Leg:	Kulu.
Feet:	Omalo, omolo, tombi.
Plate:	Dilongo.
Christian garment:	Nsombi.
jewish garment:	Nganga ndoki, ngarri ndoki.
Prescito:	Noso gonda.
To loan:	Smba.
Deep:	Sipa.
Prostitute:	Ndumba nsale.
	Yaela.
Rotten:	Mpalo.
Dust:	Tufi.
Filth:	Tina.
Chicken:	Lumelo.
Gate:	Nfumo.
Boss Father:	Tiana.

Q

Burn:	Yakp.
Want, want:	Nsolde, nkuye.
Still:	Kuako.

R

Tail:	Nkila.
Watch:	Nkunde.
Pocket protection:	Maputo.
Backing out:	Plendiensilla.
Rio Grande:	Nsondi.

Salty river: Burigna.
Red: Mbicari.
Rapa: Sao mulele.
White clothes: Bebe sinfe.

S

Saber: Kuakukuka.
Sabandija: Ngururu.
Sacerdote de Palo Monte: Tata nganga.
Saco que tenía la prenda antiguamente: Boumba.
Saco para guardar el brujo y trasladarlo: Akute songa bilongo.
Sal, salir: Mungna.
Sal de cocinar: Mpalo mungo, mensus.
Saliva: Mete.
San Antonio: Bakuende bomban.
San Francisco: Nsambi munalungo.
Santa Bárbara: Nkita.
Santo: Nsombre.
Sebo: Meba.
Pulso, argolla: Brimine.
Senos de mujer, pechos: Mañeñe.
Señorita: Maona keye.
Serpiente pitón: Mbama, ñoka.
Ser: Rala.
Sexo femenino: Marankate.
Siete rayos: Nsasi.
Soga: Musena.
Sol: Tongo, ntango.
Soldado: Meserere.
Sol naciente: Tongo yaleko.
Solo: Kaka mpe.

Sol poniente: Tongo, nfuiri.
Sortija: Nkonga sombra.
Subir: Tomoko.
Suciedad: Lumbi.

T

Tobacco: Nsungne, sunga.
Table: Momboya.
Talisman: Nkuto dilongo.
Drum: Masikila, sina, ngome.
loaded jar: Mpoka.
I am hungry: Salaina.
Testicle: Kisonga.
Land: Tato.
land of death: Nsia, fua.
All: Lulia, alonso.
Fool, cheat, liar: Iron a dakadeke, fon fon, wuari wuari.
Whirlwind: Tembo, kikongo, kilembo.
Worked: Salako, tunga.
Trunk: Musileto.
Tongo: Ntika.
Betray, change your mind: Beluka.
Thunder: Mandosi nsemo.

U

Nails: Nsala lembo.
You are married?:   Nkeye kuda.
You: Nkuye.

V

Wow nice: Lakuendako.
Come: Kuisa.
Old woman: Yuen boba, giabale.
Sweet wine: Malafo sese.
Barf: Luka.
Candle: Muinda, mpebe.
Dress: Fuata.
Old man: Nkula.
Belly: Tumbe.

Y

Yua: Lungakums.
Yucca: Madioca, mayaka mongolo, nkunia, kerelende.

Z

Shoe: Nkado.
Sapodilla: Nauru.
Bramble: Nkunia ntutu.

CHAPTER 3

PHOTOS TO ILLUSTRATE THE CONGO VOCABULARY IN CUBA.

Avianzan: Osain

Azumbo: Mountain

Anagongo: Sesame

Achiviriqui: San Miguel Arcángel

Ariongo; Suansa: River flow.

Asualo: Spirit of the River Mouth.

Bacuso: Rays

Bakasala; Engundo liri: Palm

Bandoki: Sorcerer

Banduina: Flag.

Baracuame; Burukuame: Hat

Batalla; Ofuna: Air; Wind

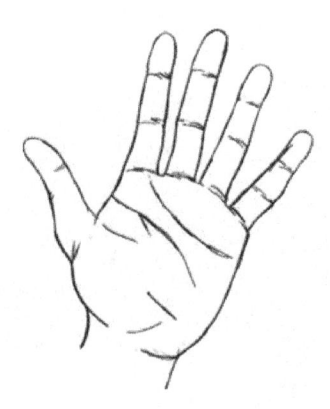

Basangal: Palm of the hand

Bebe: Lips

Bebe Sinfe: White clothes.

Bibamance: Corojo butter

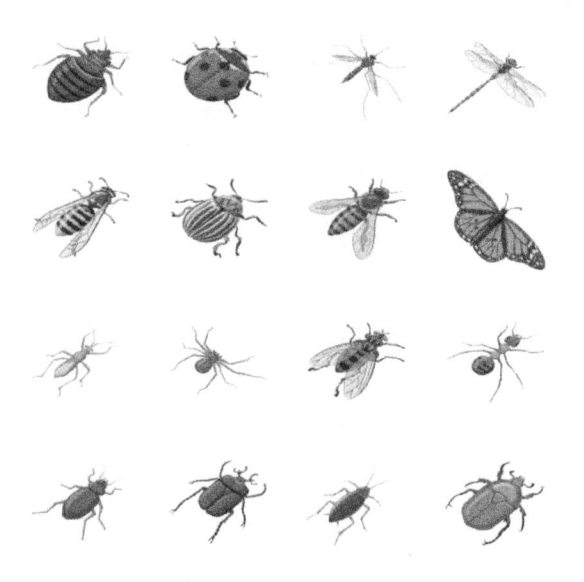

Bishishi: Bug.

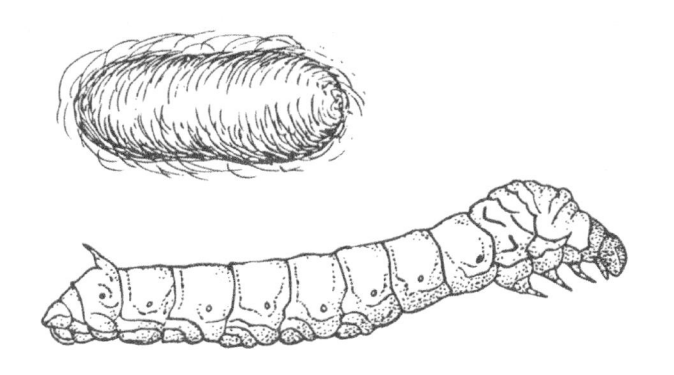

Bishishi Meko: Worm

Bilongo; Mumba: Witchcraft.

Biningulo; Engulo: Pig

Binsin sunsu: Rooster Meat

Bisi: Meat, eggs (Animals).

Lele; Wuaso:Egg.

Bisonse; Bisonse bukilanga endumba; Bisongo: Nail

Bisonse Bukilanga: Line Nail.

Bisonse ensusu: Cockspur

Bisonsi: Fish.

Bisuri; Misuri: Nose.

Boata; Entumbo: Bottle

Bobe: Kiss.

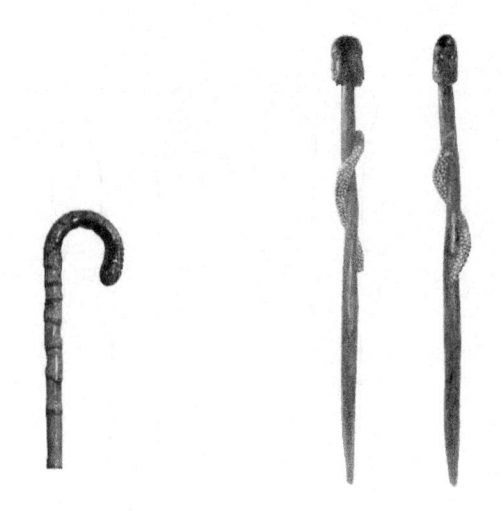

Boime: Walking stick.

Boloca: Peseta.

Bombofinda; Elefano : Elephant.

Bomba; Emboma ; Ñoka: Snake

Boma: Old snake with jars

Bomba: Jar

Bombe la Bumpar; Entuala: Cat

Bonke; Bunke; Malafo Uria: Honey

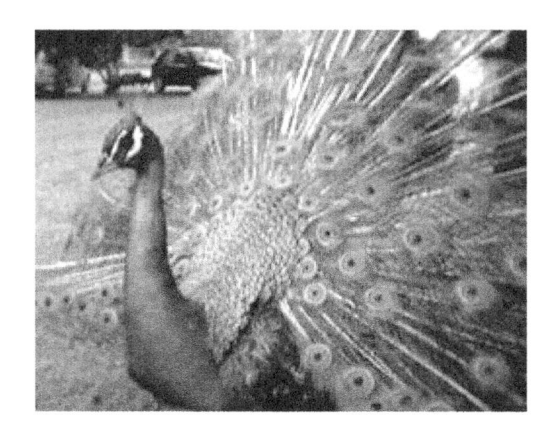

Bubococa; Ensuso mambo: Peacock

Burukuntela: fight, problem

Brankanioni: Balls, Testicles

Brimine: Pulse, Ring

Caboronda: Police

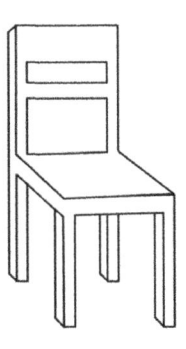

Cachicauhal: chair or seat

Cafu; Condia:: Caravel.

Calaza; Maleke: Pumpkin.

Calunga: Sea

76

Campo finda; Cotalemba: Cementery.

Camarioca: Chameleon.

Candango: Crockpot

Carcoma; Jorumina: Bibijaguas ants.

Cocoansa; Suansa: River

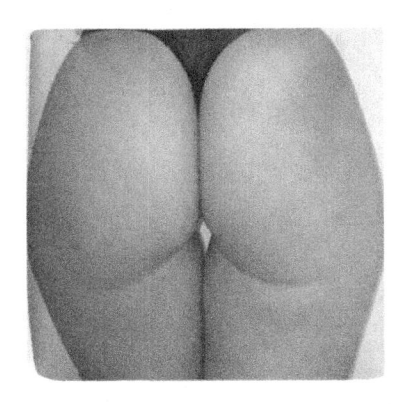

Conguso; Encombo Su; Mataca: Ass.

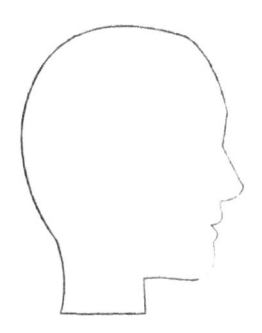

Congo: Head.

Coromina; Elana: Spider.

Cuatro vientos; Lucero Mundo; Prueba Fuerza: Elewa.

Kobayende; Chacuana Eneco; Patipuanza; Patiyaga:
Saint Lazarus

Cuco; Macaca: Coconut.

Cuile: Necklace.

Cuilo; Panguaneare: Bird.

Cuni: Stick.

Cunia; Enkunia: Tree

Cutukuonkala; Entiete; Teite: Jícara.

Cuyerere: Cocuyo (Firefly)

Chala: Spoon

Chamba; Malafo Uria Ganga: Foundation drink.

Sheshereguanco; Tocuanto: Pitirre.

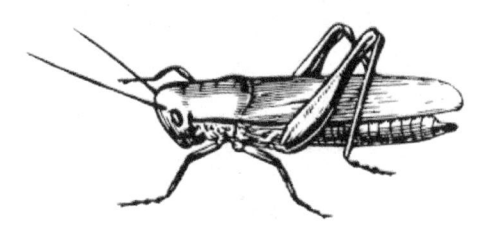

Shesheregoma: Cricket Antiagola

Shesherenguara: The Heron.

Shesheremapiango; Entosato; Teremende: Deer.

Sheshere Guanga: Tomeguín.

Chi; Ensimba: Lion.

Chicombe; Gumbembe: Jutía Conga of Cuba

Chola nguengue: Caridad del Cobre of Cuba.

Cholo;; Chula; Engando Vititi : Toad

Dialanga: Women's head scarf

Elice; Enkele: bright Star

Embele; Nbele: Bowei Knife.

Nbele Kasuso: Knife.

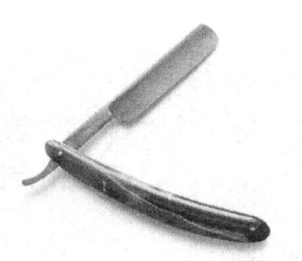

Embeleto: Razor.

Embembo: African.

Embongo: Boy, Child.

Empaka: Prepared jar.

Empolo: Powder.

Encobo: Snail.

Encombo mene: Male Goat

Encumbe: Bogie.

Encuto: Hear, ear

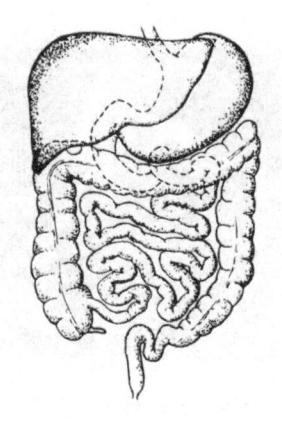

Endia: Gut.

Endundo; Endoqui: Phantom.

Endumba: Woman.

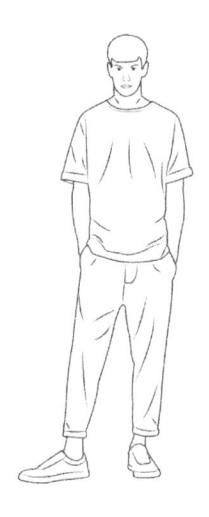

Nbelo: Men.

Enfinda; Finda: Intricate mount.

Enfita: Liana.

Enfumbe; Sance : Dead

Engando batalla; Gando Cueva: Alligator

Engo: Tiger

Engombe: Bull.

Engonda; Gonda: Moon.

Engongoro; Gongoro: Jicotea (Turtle)

Engumbiro: Centipede.

Enkegue; Encualle; Encualle: Monkeys.

Ensefo: Hair

Ensila: Path.

Ensunga: Tabacco

Ensunga mundele: Cigar

Ensuso batalla; Ofuna: Ceiba tree.

Ensuso kobayende: Guineo.

Ensuso Ligue: Guinea.

Ensuso damba: Owl.

Ensuso ganga: Rooster

Ensuso huanamburo; Ensuso suao: Duck.

Ensuso indumba: Hen.

Ensuso sambia: Pigeon.

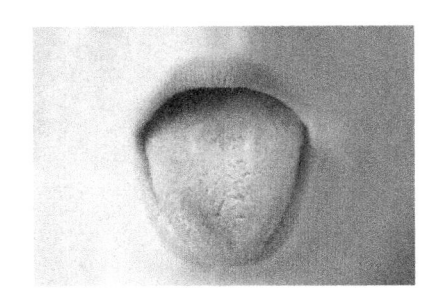

Entanda: Tongue.

Entango; Tango: Sun.

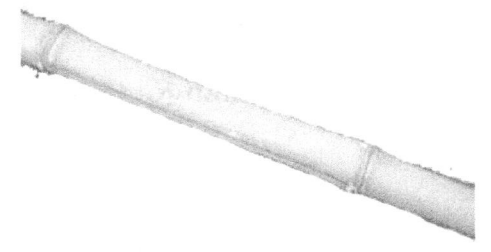

Entombre: Cane Brava.

Entufi: Shit.

Entumba Urialango: Glass

Enkoki: Arrow.

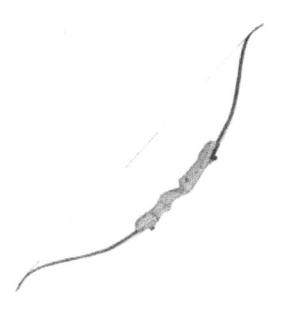

Entebo: arrow bow

Engembo; Guembo Garire: Bat

Ensosa: Chain

Falla; Lumbe: Candle

Fula: Gunpowder.

Gambula: Swirl

Gando Siro: dried guiro

Ganga: Basin casserole.

Gato: Hawk

Guandi: Soursop

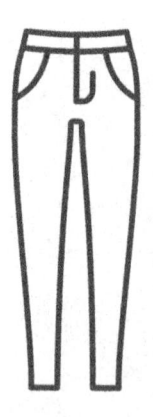

Guano: Trousers

Guao: Dog

Garbanzo

Gubasambi: Chickpea.

Caraota roja

Guba Zarabanda: Red beans.

Caraota negra

Guba Bafiote: black beans

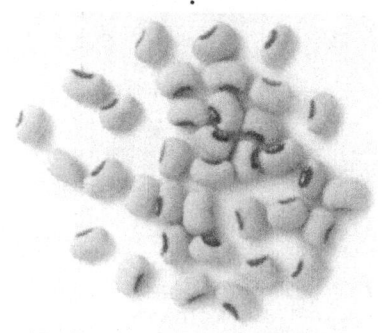

(Caritas)Frijol pico negro

Guba Kindiame: Carita.

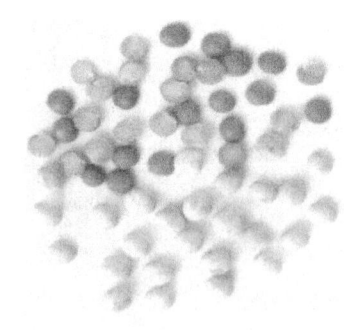

Arveja verde partida y entera

Gubatu: Pea.

Caraota blanca

Guba Mundele: White beans

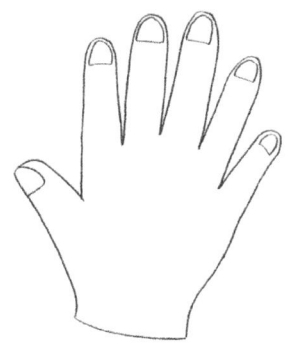

Guembo; Membo: Fingers

Gumbele: Comejen (termites).

Jole: Wood doll.

Kamakeke: Trap.

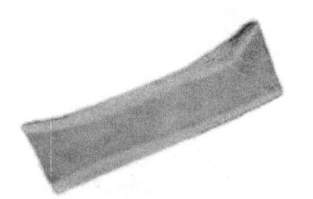

Killise: Bone.

Kindembo: Iron pot

Kotoroto: Parrot

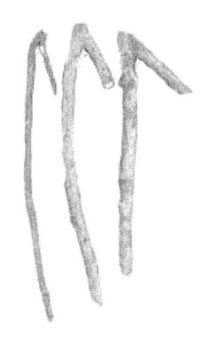

Longolla: Garabato

Lusuala: Feathers

Macujende: Guanajo (Turkey)

Macundo: Banana.

Makala cacha: Basin

Malafo sese: Dry wine.

Malafo nputo: Schnapps

Malafo Uria Balbande: Melao or molasses

Malafo Uria Sambi: Red wine.

Mamba: Water.

Mamba Kalunga: Sea water.

Lango Zambi: Water rain.

Lango NKisi: Holy Water.

Lembe: Dead

Liguena: lizard and slug

Licombola: Knee.

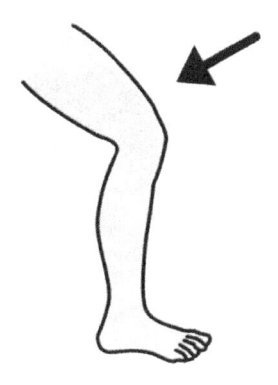

Lifangude: Leg.

Linga: have sex.

Liri: Oshosi.

Lucansi: Lucifer

Lucuana: Flowers.

Masango Nsara: Corn straw.

Masango Uria: Yellow cornmeal

Matari: Stone.

Matari Nsasi: Lightning Stone.

Mayimbe: Vulture

Mayunga: Anima Sola

Meleto: Watermelon

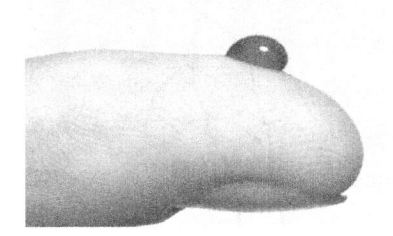

Menga: Blood.

Miapao: Bread.

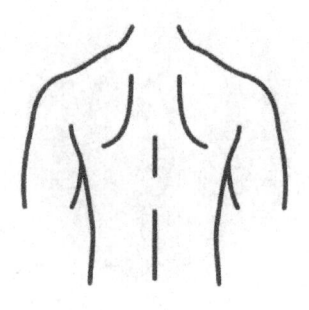

Mina: Back

Moco; Nicuaco: Hand, Arm

Mojiganga; Tegue: Shishiriku.

Monga Kalunga: Salt.

Munanguengue; Tiembla Tierra: Las Mercedes.

Munanso: House

Munanso Guanabeto; Muralla: Jail.

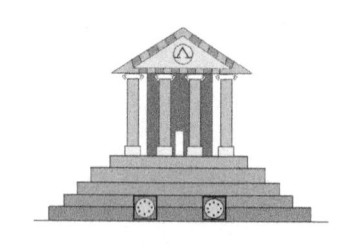

Munanso Naibola: Temple

Munanso Sambi: Church.

Munanso Uria: Bodega (grocery and liquor store in Cuba).

Munanso Uria Ngombe: Butcher shop

Munica; Terekunta: Ram.

Musenga: Sugar.

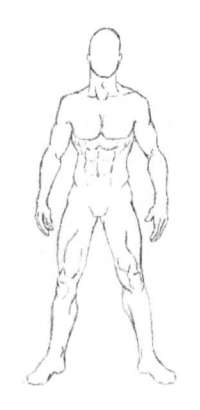

Ncembo: Body.

Nsansa; Zansa: Wood.

Osototo Mundale: Rice

Palmiche; Tilla: Broom.

Pemba Keto: Pencil.

Quimbanza: Herb.

Sambi: God.

Sambrano Sasi: 7 Rays.

Santico: Yam.

Sarabana; Zarabanda: Saint Peter.

Singoma: Drum

130

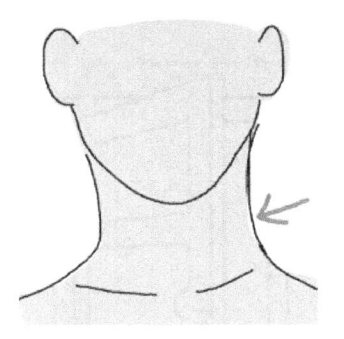

Sinkeiloca: Neck.

Somba: Frut.

Sopay: Okra.

Talankera: Door.

Tana: Orange

Tarambele: Fence; Siege

Tuine: Guasasa

Uria: Food

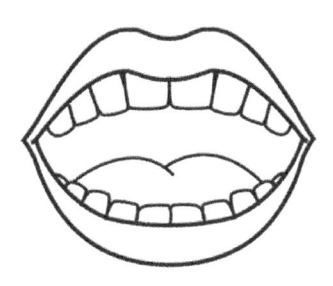

Vene: Mouth

Vueta Ngonda: Watch.

Yaba: Guava.

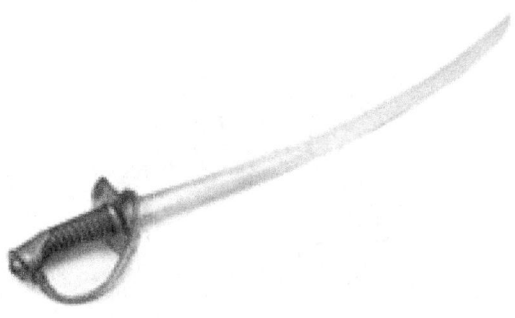

Yambele: Saber.

Zimbo: Money

Zun: Pinwheel.

Made in United States
Orlando, FL
03 March 2024